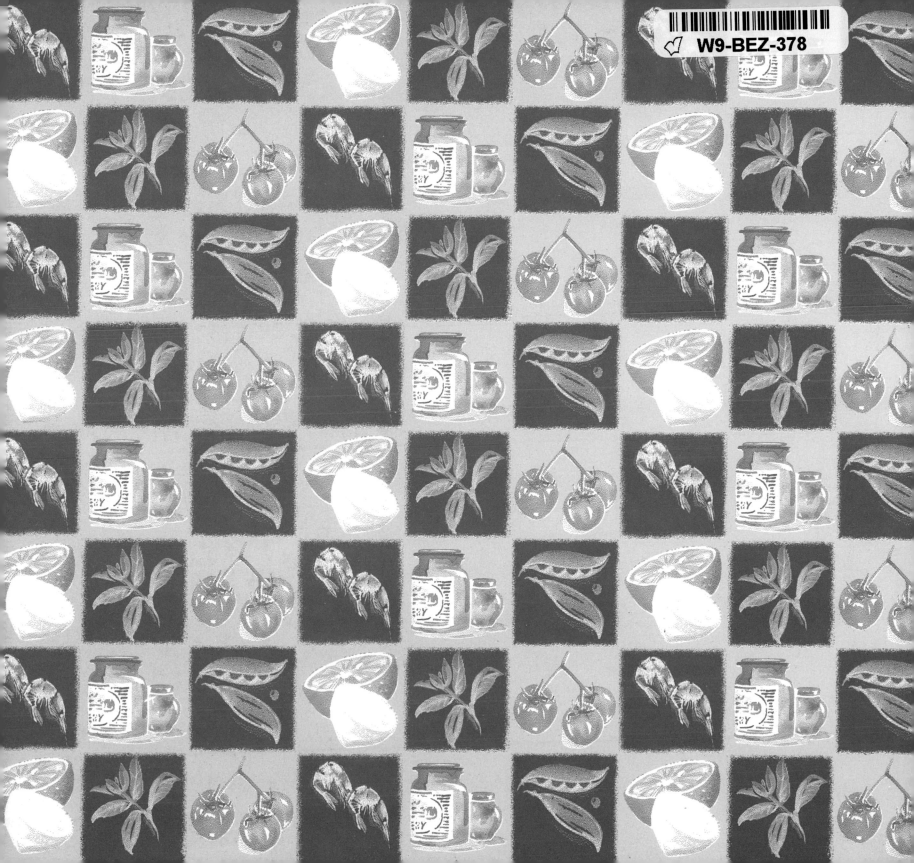

Classic

CARIBBEAN

Classic

CARIBBEAN

Delicious home cooking from the heart of the tropics

ROSAMUND GRANT

HERMES
HOUSE

This edition published by Hermes House
an imprint of Anness Publishing Limited
Hermes House, 88-89 Blackfriars Road, London SE1 8HA

Publisher Joanna Lorenz
Managing Editor Linda Fraser
Project Editor Zoe Antoniou
Designer Ian Sandom
Illustrations Madeleine David
Photography and Styling Patrick McLeavey, assisted by Rebecca Sturrock
Food for photography Joanne Craig, assisted by Curtis Edwards
Jacket photography Thomas Odulate
Production Controller Joanna King

Typeset by MC Typeset Ltd, Rochester, Kent

Printed and bound in Singapore

For all recipes, quantities are given in both metric and imperial measures, and, where appropriate,
measures are also given in standard cups and spoons. Follow one set, but not a mixture,
because they are not interchangeable.

3 5 7 9 10 8 6 4 2

Picture on frontispiece: Mango, Tomato and Red Onion Salad and Red Chilli.

CONTENTS

INTRODUCTION

LASSIC CARIBBEAN features recipes that reflect the rich diversity of traditions and cultures that have become the hallmark of the Caribbean. Many people of various races and cultures have lived in the islands and with each set of people came their traditional cooking methods and their favourite foods, which were imported. In fact, what we think of as Caribbean cooking now is actually a blend of food and cookery traditions from all over the world.

The first inhabitants of the Caribbean were the Arawak Indians who sailed from the Americas. They found many different types of fresh fruit and vegetables, such as yams, pawpaws and guavas, and introduced jerked pork to the islands themselves. The Europeans, on the other hand, who colonized the region in the early sixteenth century, experimented with the cultivation of bananas, plantains, coconut, sugar cane, oranges and limes.

When the Europeans introduced slave labour after they had exterminated the Arawaks, the eating patterns changed again. The slaves were often prevented from eating fresh fish or meat and came to depend on salted fish, which still remains immensely popular. The slaves also used spices and seasonings to add flavour to their otherwise bland food. Further influences spread after 1830, when slavery was finally abolished and plantation owners looked to the Middle East, India and China for labour, bringing in yet more cooking styles and foods.

Out of this turbulent past comes a cuisine that is colourful and versatile, imaginative and abounding in creativity. There is much to experiment with and to enjoy with family and friends, on all occasions.

This page: the Caribbean islands stretch from the coast of South America out into the Atlantic Ocean. Next page (clockwise from top left): Apple and Cinnamon Crumble Cake, Fruits of the Tropics Salad and Island Mist Fruit Punch.

INGREDIENTS

The following ingredients are most typically used in Caribbean cooking. Some may be unfamiliar, but they are all available in shops selling Caribbean foods.

ACKEE This is the fruit of an evergreen tree. The texture is soft and resembles scrambled eggs, with a slightly lemony flavour. Traditionally served with saltfish, it is also delicious with prawns or vegetables. It is available, canned, from Caribbean stores.

AUBERGINE There are many varieties: large, purple and oval-shaped, small and round, or thin and pale purple. In West Africa, the small, round, white aubergines are known as garden eggs or eggplant.

BEANS AND PEAS These include black-eyed beans, red kidney beans, black beans, pigeon peas (gunga peas) and various coloured lentils. They are often combined with rice or used in soups and stews.

CASSAVA This tropical root vegetable originated in Brazil. It is a long, irregularly shaped root vegetable with a rough brown skin and hard, white starchy flesh. A popular vegetable in the Caribbean, it can be eaten boiled, baked or fried.

CHRISTOPHENE Also known as chocho or chayote, this pear-shaped vegetable has a bland flavour and is similar in texture to squash. It is cooked and used as a side dish or in soups.

COCONUT This is a large one-seeded nut of the coconut palm tree. The mature coconut has a hairy outer shell which contains sweet, thick white flesh, from which coconut milk is extracted. Chop into small pieces, then liquidize with a little water and press through a sieve to extract the milk.

Clockwise from top left: okra, christophene, baby aubergines, aubergine, garden eggs and ackee.

CORNMEAL Cornmeal is made from dried, ground corn kernels. The type most commonly used is yellow – either fine or coarse-grained. Cornmeal can be used to make cakes, breads and porridge, or as a coating when frying fish or chicken.

CREAMED COCONUT Creamed coconut can be bought in 200g/7oz packets from most supermarkets, grocery and health food shops. The coconut can be stored for several weeks in the fridge.

DHAL In the Caribbean, this is a spicy soup made from split peas or lentils. Dhal puri (roti) is an unleavened bread.

EDDOE OR COCO A small globular root vegetable. The flesh is white and starchy like potato and, after peeling, it can be boiled and served as an accompaniment or used in soups.

GREEN BANANAS Only certain varieties are used in cooking. They are usually boiled, with or without their skins.

GUAVA The pale yellow edible skin covers rose-pink succulent flesh, which in turn covers a seed-laden soft pulp. Guavas have a slightly spicy smell and are used to make jam or added to fruit salads.

HERB SEASONING Pound 4 chopped spring onions, 1 garlic clove, 15ml/1 tbsp each fresh, or 5ml/1 tsp dried, thyme and basil with 15ml/1 tbsp fresh coriander, in a mortar until smooth.

MANGOES Mangoes come in a variety of shapes, sizes, colours and textures. Unripe, they are green, turning yellow, pink or crimson-green as they ripen. For desserts, jellies or jams, make sure the fruit is ripe – it should feel pliable to the touch without being too spongy. Unripe green mangoes are used for chutney, curries and stews.

OKRA Choose small, firm ones. Wash and dry them before trimming and cutting to prevent them from getting too sticky.

PEPPERS The family of peppers includes both hot and sweet types, and there are many varieties of hot peppers, or chillies. Fresh chillies can be green, red or yellow. The seeds and core are the hottest part and can be removed before use, under cold running water. A range of peppers is grown in the Caribbean and one of the hottest is the Scotch Bonnet chilli. It is best to wear gloves when preparing chillies and take care not to rub your eyes afterwards.

PLANTAINS These belong to the banana family. They are inedible raw and must be cooked before eating. They can be green, yellow or very dark according to ripeness and can be roasted, boiled, mashed and fried. Plantains can be eaten as an appetizer, in soups, as a vegetable or in desserts.

SALTFISH OR SALT COD Of all the saltfish, cod has the best flavour. To remove the salt, wash the fish and soak it for several hours in cold water. Remove the fish to clean water and boil for 15–20 minutes.

Drain off the water and flake the fish, discarding the skin and bones.

SNAPPER OR RED FISH A silver, pinkish-red fish with firm white flesh, snapper is imported in small or large sizes from approximately 225g–1.5kg/8oz–3lb. Snapper can be fried, baked, steamed or boiled.

SPICE SEASONING Mix 15ml/1 tbsp garlic granules, 7.5ml/½ tbsp coarse grain black pepper, 7.5ml/½ tbsp each paprika, celery salt and curry powder with 5ml/1 tsp caster sugar. Store in a dry container, ready for use when needed.

SWEET POTATO The skin of this vegetable ranges in colour from white to pink to reddish-brown. The white-fleshed, red-skinned variety is most commonly used in Caribbean cooking. Sweet potatoes can be boiled, roasted, fried, creamed or baked in their skins. They are used in sweet and savoury dishes.

YAM These come in all sizes, so when buying ask for a piece the size you need. The flesh is either yellow or white and can be eaten boiled, roasted, baked, mashed or made into chips.

Picture shows (clockwise from top left): cassava, eddoes, orange sweet potatoes, white yam and white sweet potatoes.

LAMB AND LENTIL SOUP

ou can add as many vegetables as you like to this wholesome dish to make a "bigger" soup.

INGREDIENTS
1.5 litres/2½ pints/6¼ cups water
or stock
900g/2lb neck of lamb, cut into chops
½ onion, chopped
1 garlic clove, crushed
1 bay leaf
1 clove
2 thyme sprigs
225g/8oz potatoes
175g/6oz/¾ cup red lentils
600ml/1 pint/2½ cups water
salt and freshly ground black pepper
parsley, to garnish

SERVES 4

1 Put the water or stock and meat in a large saucepan with the onion, garlic, bay leaf, clove and thyme sprigs. Bring to the boil and simmer for about 1 hour, or until the lamb is tender.

2 Cut the potatoes into 2.5cm/1in pieces and add them to the saucepan.

3 Add the lentils to the saucepan and season the soup with a little salt and plenty of black pepper.

4 Add 300ml/½ pint/1¼ cups water, or more if the soup becomes too thick, to come just above the surface of the meat and vegetables. Cover and simmer gently for about 25 minutes, or until the lentils are cooked and well blended into the soup. Just before serving, sprinkle in the parsley and stir well.

FISH AND SWEET POTATO SOUP

The subtle sweetness of the potato combined with the fish and the aromatic flavour of oregano, makes this an appetizing soup.

INGREDIENTS
½ onion, chopped
175g/6oz sweet potato, peeled and diced
175g/6oz boneless white fish
fillet, skinned
50g/2oz carrot, chopped
5ml/1 tsp chopped fresh oregano or
2.5ml/½ tsp dried
2.5ml/½ tsp ground cinnamon
1.35 litres/2¼ pints/5½ cups fish stock
75ml/5 tbsp single cream
chopped fresh parsley, to garnish

SERVES 4

1 Put the onion, sweet potato, fish, carrot, oregano, cinnamon and half of the stock in a saucepan. Bring to the boil, then simmer for 20 minutes or until the potatoes are cooked.

2 Leave the fish and vegetables with their liquid in the saucepan until they have cooled down slightly, then pour them very carefully into a blender or food processor. Blend the mixture together until it becomes a smooth soup-like purée.

3 Return the soup to the saucepan, then add the remaining stock and gently bring to the boil. Reduce the heat to low and add the single cream, then gently heat through without boiling. Serve hot, garnished with the chopped parsley.

CARIBBEAN VEGETABLE SOUP

This vegetable soup is refreshing and filling and good as a main course for lunch. Cooked meat and fish can also be added, if liked.

INGREDIENTS
25g/1oz/2 tbsp butter or margarine
1 onion, chopped
1 garlic clove, crushed
2 carrots, sliced
1.5 litres/2¹⁄₂ pints/6¹⁄₄ cups
vegetable stock
2 bay leaves
2 thyme sprigs
1 celery stick, finely chopped
2 green bananas, peeled and cut into 4
175g/6oz white yam or eddoe,
peeled and cubed
25g/1oz/2 tbsp red lentils
1 christophene, peeled and chopped
25g/1oz/2 tbsp macaroni (optional)
salt and freshly ground black pepper
chopped spring onions, to garnish

SERVES 4

COOK'S TIP
Use other root vegetables or potatoes if yam or eddoes are not available. Add more stock for a thinner soup.

1 Melt the butter or margarine in a saucepan and fry the onion, garlic and carrots for a few minutes, stirring occasionally. Add the stock, bay leaves and thyme and bring to the boil.

2 Add the celery, green bananas, white yam or eddoe, lentils, christophene and macaroni, if using. Season and simmer for 25 minutes, or until the vegetables are cooked. Serve garnished with spring onions.

CRAB CAKES WITH TOMATO DIP

hese are quite delicious and they are just as good when made with canned tuna fish, too.

INGREDIENTS
225g/8oz white crab meat
115g/4oz/1⅓ cup cooked
potatoes, mashed
25g/1oz/2 tbsp fresh herb seasoning
2.5ml/½ tsp mild mustard
2.5ml/½ tsp freshly ground black pepper
½ hot chilli pepper
15ml/1 tbsp shrimp paste (optional)
2.5ml/½ tsp dried oregano, crushed
1 egg white, beaten
flour, for dusting
oil, for frying
lime wedges and basil leaves, to garnish

FOR THE TOMATO DIP
15ml/1 tbsp butter or margarine
½ onion, finely chopped
2 canned plum tomatoes, chopped
1 garlic clove, crushed
150ml/¼ pint/⅔ cup water
5–10ml/1–2 tsp malt vinegar
15ml/1 tbsp chopped fresh coriander
½ hot chilli pepper, chopped

MAKES ABOUT 15

1 To make the crab cakes, mix together the crab meat, potatoes, herb seasoning, mustard, pepper, hot chilli pepper, shrimp paste, if using, oregano and egg in a large bowl. Chill for 30 minutes to allow the flavours to blend, and to help the mixture bind together.

2 To make the tomato dip, melt the butter or margarine in a small pan. Add the onion, tomato and garlic and sauté for about 5 minutes until the onion is soft.

3 Add the water, vinegar, coriander and hot pepper. Simmer for 10 minutes.

4 Pour the tomato liquid into a food processor or blender and blend to a smooth purée. Pour into a bowl and either keep warm or chill as required.

5 Using a spoon, shape the mixture into rounds and dust with flour. Heat a little oil in a frying pan and fry the crab cakes a few at a time for 2–3 minutes on each side until they turn golden brown.

6 Drain on kitchen paper and keep the crab cakes warm while cooking the remaining cakes. Garnish with lime wedges and basil leaves and serve with the tomato dip.

SALTFISH FRITTERS

hese delicious fritters are also known as *Accras*. Eat them as a starter or as a tasty snack.

INGREDIENTS

115g/4oz/1 cup self-raising flour
115g/4oz/1 cup plain flour
2.5ml/^{1}/$_2$ tsp baking powder
175g/6oz soaked salt cod, shredded
1 egg, whisked
15ml/1 tbsp chopped spring onion
1 garlic clove, crushed
2.5ml/^{1}/$_2$ tsp freshly ground black pepper
^{1}/$_2$ hot chilli pepper, seeded and finely chopped
1.5ml/^{1}/$_4$ tsp turmeric
45ml/3 tbsp milk
vegetable oil, for shallow frying

MAKES 15

1 Sift the flours and baking powder together, then add the salt cod, egg, spring onion, garlic, pepper, hot pepper and turmeric. Add some of the milk and mix.

2 Gradually stir in the remaining milk, adding just enough to make a thick batter. Stir thoroughly so that all the ingredients are combined.

3 Heat a little vegetable oil in a large frying pan until it is very hot. Add spoonfuls of the salt cod mixture and fry for a few minutes on each side until they are golden brown and puffy. Lift out the fritters, drain well on kitchen paper and keep them warm while cooking the rest of the mixture in the same way. Serve the fritters either hot or cold, as a snack.

SPINACH PATTIES

hese are a delicious vegetarian version of the more traditional minced meat patties.

INGREDIENTS
FOR THE PASTRY
225g/8oz/2 cups plain flour
115g/4oz/¹/₂ cup butter or margarine,
chilled and diced
1 egg yolk
milk, to glaze

FOR THE FILLING
25g/1oz/2 tbsp butter or margarine
1 small onion, finely chopped
175–225g/6–8oz fresh or frozen leaf
spinach, chopped
2.5ml/¹/₂ tsp ground cumin
¹/₂ vegetable stock cube, crumbled
freshly ground black pepper

MAKES 10–12

1 Preheat the oven to 200°C/400°F/Gas 6. Lightly grease a muffin tin.

2 For the filling, melt the butter or margarine in a saucepan, add the onion and cook until soft. Stir in the spinach, cumin, stock cube and pepper, and cook for about 5 minutes. Leave to cool.

3 To make the pastry, put the flour in a bowl and rub in the butter or margarine until the mixture resembles breadcrumbs. Add the egg yolk and 30–45ml/2–3 tbsp cold water and mix to a firm dough. Turn out the pastry on to a floured surface.

4 Knead the dough for a few seconds, then divide it in half and roll out one half to a square or rectangle. Cut out 10–12 rounds using a 9cm/3¹/₂in pastry cutter. Press these into the hollows of the prepared tin. Roll out the remaining dough and cut out slightly smaller rounds to cover the patties.

5 Spoon about 15ml/1 tbsp of the spinach mixture into the pastry cases. Add on the pastry lids, press the edges with a fork to seal them and prick the tops with the fork. Brush with milk and bake for 15–20 minutes until golden brown. Serve hot or cold.

Spinach Plantain Rounds

his delectable way of serving plantains is a little fiddly to make, but well worth it! The plantains must be ripe, but still firm.

Ingredients

2 large ripe plantains
vegetable oil, for frying
25g/1oz/2 tbsp butter or margarine
25g/1oz/2 tbsp finely chopped onion
2 garlic cloves, crushed
450g/1lb fresh spinach, chopped
pinch of freshly grated nutmeg
1 egg, beaten
wholemeal flour, for dusting
salt and freshly ground black pepper

Serves 4

1 Using a small, sharp knife, cut each plantain lengthways into four slices.

2 Heat a little vegetable oil in a large frying pan and fry the plantain slices on both sides until they are lightly golden brown but not fully cooked. Drain them well on kitchen paper and reserve the oil.

3 Melt the butter or margarine in a saucepan and sauté the chopped onion and garlic for a few minutes, or until the onion is soft.

4 Add the chopped spinach, salt, black pepper and grated nutmeg. Cover and cook for about 5 minutes until the spinach has reduced. Cool, then tip into a sieve and press out any excess moisture.

5 Curl the plantain slices into rings and secure each ring with half a wooden cocktail stick. Pack each plantain ring with a little of the cooked spinach mixture.

6 Place the egg and flour in two separate shallow dishes. Add a little more oil to the frying pan, if necessary, and heat until it is moderately hot. Dip the plantain rings in the egg and then in the flour and fry on both sides for 1–2 minutes until golden brown.

7 Drain the plantain rounds on kitchen paper and serve them hot or cold with a salad, or as part of a meal.

Cook's Tip
If fresh spinach is not available, you can use frozen spinach, thawed and thoroughly drained.
The plantain rings can be small or large and, if preferred, minced meat, mashed fish or beans can be used instead of spinach for the filling.

OKRA FRIED RICE

egetarians are spoilt for choice in the Caribbean and this dish is another example of the wide choice of dishes available. It can be enjoyed as a side dish or as a light meal on its own.

INGREDIENTS
30ml/2 tbsp vegetable oil
15ml/1 tbsp butter or margarine
1 garlic clove, crushed
¹⁄₂ red onion, finely chopped
115g/4oz okra, topped and tailed
30ml/2 tbsp diced green and red peppers
2.5ml/¹⁄₂ tsp dried thyme
2 green chillies, finely chopped
2.5ml/¹⁄₂ tsp five-spice powder
1 vegetable stock cube
30ml/2 tbsp soy sauce
15ml/1 tbsp chopped fresh coriander
225g/8oz/2¹⁄₂ cups boiled rice
salt and freshly ground black pepper
coriander sprigs, to garnish

SERVES 3–4

1 Heat the vegetable oil and butter or margarine in a large frying pan or wok. Add the garlic and red onion and cook over a moderate heat for about 5 minutes, or until the onion is soft.

2 Thinly slice the okra, add to the pan or wok and sauté gently for 6–7 minutes.

3 Add the diced green and red peppers, dried thyme, green chillies and the five-spice powder to the wok or frying pan. Cook for about 3 minutes, stirring together. Crumble the vegetable stock cube into the mixture and stir well.

4 Add the soy sauce, fresh coriander and boiled rice and heat through, stirring well. Season with salt and freshly ground black pepper to taste. Serve hot, garnished with coriander sprigs.

AUBERGINES STUFFED WITH SWEET POTATO

he combination of sweet potato and aubergine makes this a particularly attractive dish. You can find sweet potato in many ethnic shops as well as most big supermarkets.

INGREDIENTS

225g/8oz sweet potatoes, peeled
2.5ml/¹/₂ tsp chopped fresh thyme
75g/3oz Cheddar cheese, diced
25g/1oz/2 tbsp chopped spring onion
15ml/1 tbsp each chopped red
and green pepper
1 garlic clove, crushed
2 large aubergines
30ml/2 tbsp plain flour
15ml/1 tbsp spice seasoning
olive oil, for frying
2 tomatoes, sliced
salt and freshly ground black pepper
chopped fresh parsley, to garnish

SERVES 3–4

1 Preheat the oven to 180°C/350°F/Gas 4. Cook the sweet potatoes until they are tender, then drain them well. Place them in a bowl and mash.

2 Add the fresh thyme, Cheddar cheese, spring onion, red and green peppers, garlic and salt and pepper and mix well.

3 Cut each aubergine lengthways into four slices. Mix the flour and spice seasoning together and dust over each slice. Heat a little olive oil in a large frying pan and fry until just browned. Drain well and cool. Spoon a little of the potato mixture into the middle of each slice and roll up.

4 Butter two large pieces of cooking foil and place four rolls on each. Add slices of tomato, wrap up the parcels and bake for 20 minutes in the oven. Serve the rolls hot, garnished with plenty of fresh parsley.

RED BEAN CHILLI

his vegetarian chilli can be adapted to accommodate meat-eaters by adding either minced beef or lamb in place of the lentils. Add the meat once the onions are soft, and fry until nicely browned before adding the tomatoes.

INGREDIENTS
30ml/2 tbsp vegetable oil
1 onion, chopped
400g/14oz can chopped tomatoes
2 garlic cloves, crushed
300ml/¹/₂ pint/1¹/₄ cups white wine
300ml/¹/₂ pint/1¹/₄ cups vegetable stock
115g/4oz/¹/₂ cup red lentils
2 thyme sprigs or 5ml/1 tsp dried thyme
10ml/2 tsp ground cumin
45ml/3 tbsp dark soy sauce
¹/₂ hot chilli pepper, finely chopped
5ml/1 tsp mixed spice
15ml/1 tbsp oyster sauce (optional)
225g/8oz can red kidney beans, drained
10ml/2 tsp sugar
salt
boiled rice and sweetcorn kernels, to serve

SERVES 4

1 Heat the oil in a large saucepan and fry the onion over a moderate heat for a few minutes, until slightly softened. Add the chopped tomatoes and garlic and cook for 10 minutes. Stir in the white wine and vegetable stock.

2 Add the red lentils, thyme, ground cumin, soy sauce, hot chilli pepper, mixed spice and oyster sauce, if using, and stir well.

COOK'S TIP
Fiery chillies can irritate the skin, so always wash your hands well after handling them and take care not to touch your eyes. If you like really hot, spicy food then add the seeds from the chilli too.

3 Cover and simmer for 40 minutes, or until the lentils are cooked, stirring occasionally and adding a little water if the lentils begin to dry out.

4 Stir in the red kidney beans and sugar and continue cooking for 10 minutes, adding a little extra vegetable stock or water, if necessary. Season to taste with salt and serve hot with plenty of boiled rice and sweetcorn kernels.

MANGO, TOMATO AND RED ONION SALAD

This salad makes an appetizing starter. The under-ripe mango has a subtle sweetness and the flavour blends very well with the tomato.

INGREDIENTS
1 firm under-ripe mango
2 large tomatoes or 1 beefsteak
tomato, sliced
¹/₂ red onion, sliced into rings
¹/₂ cucumber, peeled and thinly sliced
30ml/2 tbsp sunflower or vegetable oil
15ml/1 tbsp lemon juice
1 garlic clove, crushed
2.5ml/¹/₂ tsp hot pepper sauce
sugar, to taste
salt and freshly ground black pepper
snipped chives, to garnish

SERVES 4

1 Cut away two thick slices from either side of the mango stone and cut them into slices. Peel the skin from the slices.

2 Arrange the mango, tomato, onion and cucumber slices on a large serving plate.

3 Blend the oil, lemon juice, garlic, hot pepper sauce, salt and black pepper in a blender or food processor, or place in a small jar and shake vigorously. Add a pinch of sugar to taste and mix again.

4 Pour the dressing over the salad and garnish with snipped chives. Serve at room temperature or chilled. This salad makes a refreshing and light accompaniment to many dishes, as well as a delicious starter.

ACKEE WITH MUSHROOMS

ckee is a fruit with a soft texture and a slightly lemony flavour that adds a subtle taste to most vegetables.

INGREDIENTS
25g/1oz/2 tbsp butter or margarine
30ml/2 tbsp vegetable oil
1 onion, chopped
2 garlic cloves, crushed
2 canned plum tomatoes, plus
30ml/2 tbsp of the tomato juice
¹/₂ red pepper, chopped
1 hot chilli pepper, chopped (optional)
175g/6oz mushrooms, chopped
540g/1lb 6oz can ackee, drained
15ml/1 tbsp chopped fresh parsley
salt
150ml/¹/₄ pint/²/₃ cup vegetable stock
chopped fresh parsley and coriander
sprigs, to garnish
boiled rice, to serve

SERVES 4

1 Heat the butter or margarine and vegetable oil in a large frying pan, add the onion and garlic and sauté for a few minutes over a moderate heat until the onion has softened.

2 Add the canned tomatoes, tomato juice, red pepper, hot chilli pepper, if using, mushrooms, ackee and parsley and season with salt to taste.

3 Stir gently, pour in the stock and slowly bring to the boil. Reduce the heat and simmer for 5 minutes. Garnish with parsley and coriander and serve with rice.

COOK'S TIP
Use a metal spoon or fork to mix the ingredients carefully as ackee breaks up very easily.

CREOLE FISH STEW

In many Caribbean dishes, fish is seasoned with herbs and spices and, as in this recipe, it is often left to marinate for a fuller flavour.

INGREDIENTS
30ml/2 tbsp spice seasoning
30ml/2 tbsp malt vinegar
2 whole red bream or large snapper,
prepared and cut into 2.5cm/1in pieces
flour, for dusting
oil, for frying

FOR THE SAUCE
30ml/2 tbsp vegetable oil
15ml/1 tbsp butter or margarine
1 onion, finely chopped
275g/10oz fresh tomatoes, peeled and
finely chopped
2 garlic cloves, crushed
2 thyme sprigs
600ml/1 pint/2½ cups fish stock or water
2.5ml/½ tsp ground cinnamon
1 hot chilli pepper, chopped
115g/4oz each red and green pepper,
finely chopped
salt
oregano sprigs, to garnish

SERVES 4–6

1 Sprinkle the spice seasoning and vinegar over the fish, turning to coat. Set aside to marinate for at least 2 hours or overnight in the fridge.

2 When ready to cook, place a little flour on a large plate and coat the fish pieces, shaking off any excess flour.

3 Heat a little oil in a large frying pan and fry the fish pieces for about 5 minutes until golden brown, then set aside. Don't worry if the fish is not cooked through as it will finish cooking in the sauce.

4 To make the sauce, heat the oil and butter or margarine in a large frying pan or wok and stir-fry the onion for 5 minutes. Add the tomatoes, garlic and thyme, stir and simmer for 5 minutes more. Stir in the stock or water, cinnamon and hot pepper.

5 Add the fish pieces and the chopped peppers. Simmer until the fish is cooked through and the stock has reduced to a thick sauce. Adjust the seasoning with salt. Serve hot, garnished with oregano sprigs.

SALMON IN MANGO AND GINGER SAUCE

Mango and salmon complement each other, especially with the subtle flavour of tarragon.

INGREDIENTS

2 salmon steaks (about 275g/10oz each)
a little lemon juice
1–2 garlic cloves, crushed
5ml/1 tsp dried tarragon, crushed
2 shallots, roughly chopped
1 tomato, roughly chopped
1 ripe mango (about
175g/6oz flesh), chopped
150ml/¼ pint/⅔ cup fish stock or water
15ml/1 tbsp ginger syrup
25g/1oz/2 tbsp butter
salt and freshly ground black pepper

SERVES 2

1 Place the salmon steaks in a shallow dish and season with the lemon juice, garlic, tarragon and salt and pepper. Set aside in the fridge to marinate for at least 1 hour.

2 Meanwhile, place the shallots, tomato and mango in a blender or food processor and blend until smooth. Add the fish stock or water and the ginger syrup, blend again and set aside.

3 Melt the butter in a frying pan and sauté the marinated salmon steaks for about 5 minutes on each side.

4 Add the mango purée to the frying pan, cover and simmer gently until the salmon steaks are cooked through.

5 Transfer the salmon steaks to warmed serving plates. Make sure the mango sauce is hot and adjust the seasoning to taste. Pour the hot sauce over the salmon steaks and serve immediately.

COCONUT KING PRAWNS WITH CRISPS

If large raw prawns are difficult to obtain, use cooked prawns instead. However, raw prawns absorb more flavour from the marinade, so they are the ideal choice. This dish is best served with Plantain and Sweet Potato Crisps.

INGREDIENTS
12 large raw prawns
2 garlic cloves, crushed
15ml/1 tbsp lemon juice
50g/2oz/4 tbsp fine desiccated coconut
25g/1oz/2 tbsp snipped fresh chives
150ml/¼ pint/⅔ cup milk
2 eggs, beaten
oil, for deep frying
salt and freshly ground black pepper
lime or lemon wedges and
flat leaf parsley, to garnish

SERVES 3–4

1 Peel and devein the prawns, leaving the tails intact, then cut the prawns along the length of their backs without cutting right through and fan them out. Rinse under cold water and pat dry.

2 Blend the garlic, lemon juice and seasoning in a shallow dish, then add the prawns and marinate for about 1 hour.

3 Mix together the coconut and chives in a shallow dish, and put the milk and eggs in two separate dishes. Dip each prawn into the milk, then into the beaten egg and finally into the coconut and chive mixture.

4 Heat the oil in a large pan or deep-fat fryer and fry the prawns for 1 minute until golden, then drain. Serve hot garnished with lime or lemon wedges and parsley.

COOK'S TIP
Plantain and Sweet Potato Crisps make a delicious accompaniment to this or any Caribbean dish.
Remove the skin of the plantains (green ones if possible), by cutting each end and slicing them lengthways so that they can be lifted away from the skin. Place in cold salted water to prevent them from discolouring. Peel the sweet potato under cold water and add to the plantains. While you are heating some oil in a deep-fat fryer, dry the vegetables and slice into thin rounds. Fry until crisp. Drain and transfer them to a dish lined with kitchen paper. Sprinkle with salt and leave the crisps to cool.

KING PRAWNS IN SWEETCORN SAUCE

his sauce makes a hearty filling for baked sweet potatoes. Bake the potatoes for about 45 minutes, or until they are soft to the touch and begin to caramelize. Liquid will seep through the skin slightly.

INGREDIENTS

24–30 large raw prawns
juice of 1 lemon
spice seasoning, for dusting
25g/1oz/2 tbsp butter or margarine
1 onion, chopped
2 garlic cloves, crushed
30ml/2 tbsp tomato purée
2.5ml/½ tsp dried thyme
2.5ml/½ tsp ground cinnamon
15ml/1 tbsp chopped fresh coriander
½ hot chilli pepper, chopped
175g/6oz frozen or canned sweetcorn
300ml/½ pint/1¼ cups coconut milk
chopped fresh coriander, to garnish

SERVES 4

COOK'S TIP
If you use raw king prawns, make a stock from the shells and use in place of some of the coconut milk.

---

1 Sprinkle the raw prawns with lemon juice and spice seasoning and leave to marinate in a cool place for 1 hour.

2 Melt the butter or margarine in a saucepan, and fry the onion and garlic for 5 minutes, until slightly softened.

3 Add the marinated prawns to the pan and cook for a few minutes, stirring occasionally until they are cooked through and pink. Transfer the prawns, onion and garlic to a bowl, leaving behind some of the buttery liquid.

4 Add the tomato purée to the pan and cook over a low heat, stirring thoroughly. Add the thyme, cinnamon, coriander and hot pepper and stir well.

5 Blend the sweetcorn (reserving about 15ml/1 tbsp) in a blender or food processor with the coconut milk. Add to the pan and simmer until reduced. Add the prawns and reserved sweetcorn, and simmer for about 5 minutes. Serve hot, garnished with chopped fresh coriander.

FRIED SNAPPER WITH AVOCADO

C aribbean fried fish is often eaten with Fried Dumplins or hard-dough bread and, as in this recipe, it is sometimes accompanied by avocado – this makes a delicious light supper or lunch.

INGREDIENTS
1 lemon
4 red snappers, about 225g/8oz each, prepared
10ml/2 tsp spice seasoning
flour, for dusting
oil, for frying
chopped fresh parsley and lime slices, to garnish
2 avocados and slices of corn on the cob, to serve

SERVES 4

1 Squeeze the lemon juice over the inside and outside of the fish and sprinkle them all over with the spice seasoning. Set the fish aside in a shallow dish to marinate in a cool place for a few hours.

2 Lift the fish out of the dish and dust it with the flour, shaking off any excess.

3 Heat the oil in a non-stick pan over a moderate heat. Add the fish and fry for about 10 minutes on each side until browned and crispy.

4 Halve the avocados, remove the stones and cut in half again. Peel away the skin and cut the flesh into thin strips.

5 Place the fried fish on warmed serving plates with the avocado and corn slices. Serve the dish hot, garnished with fresh parsley and lime slices.

FILLETS OF TROUT IN WINE SAUCE WITH PLANTAIN

Tropical fish would add a distinctive flavour to this dish, but any filleted white fish can be cooked in this way, if you like.

INGREDIENTS
4 trout fillets
spice seasoning, for dusting
25g/1oz/2 tbsp butter or margarine
1–2 garlic cloves
150ml/¼ pint/⅔ cup white wine
150ml/¼ pint/⅔ cup fish stock
10ml/2 tsp honey
15–30ml/1–2 tbsp chopped fresh parsley
1 yellow plantain
oil, for frying
salt and freshly ground black pepper

SERVES 4

COOK'S TIP
Plantains belong to the banana family and they can be green, yellow or brown, depending on ripeness. Unlike bananas, plantains must be cooked and their subtle flavour is particularly effective in spicy dishes.

1 Season the trout fillets with the spice seasoning and marinate for 1 hour.

2 Melt the butter or margarine in a large frying pan and heat gently for 1 minute. Add the trout fillets and sauté for 5 minutes, or until cooked through, turning carefully once. Transfer the fillets to a plate and keep warm.

3 Add the garlic, wine, fish stock and honey to the saucepan, bring to the boil and simmer to reduce the liquid slightly. Return the trout fillets to the pan and spoon over the sauce. Sprinkle with parsley and simmer gently for a few minutes.

4 Meanwhile, peel the plantain and cut it into rounds. Heat a little oil in a frying pan and fry the plantain slices for a few minutes, until golden brown, turning once only. Transfer the trout fillets to warmed serving plates. Stir the sauce, adjust the seasoning and pour over the fish. Serve with the fried plantain.

ESCHOVISHED FISH

This dish is of Spanish origin and is very popular throughout the Caribbean. There are as many variations of the name of the dish as there are ways of preparing it.

INGREDIENTS
900g/2lb cod fillet
juice of ¹/₂ lemon
15ml/1 tbsp spice seasoning
flour, for dusting
oil, for frying
lemon wedges, to garnish

FOR THE SAUCE
30ml/2 tbsp vegetable oil
1 onion, sliced
¹/₂ red pepper, sliced
¹/₂ christophene, peeled and seeded,
cut into small pieces
2 garlic cloves, crushed
120ml/4fl oz/¹/₂ cup malt vinegar
75ml/5 tbsp water
2.5ml/¹/₂ tsp ground allspice
1 bay leaf
1 small Scotch Bonnet chilli, chopped
15ml/1 tbsp soft brown sugar
salt and freshly ground black pepper

SERVES 4–6

1 Place the cod fillet in a shallow dish and squeeze over the lemon juice, then sprinkle it with the spice seasoning and pat it into the fish. Leave to marinate in a cool place for at least 1 hour.

2 Cut the fish into 7.5cm/3in pieces and dust it with a little flour, shaking off any of the excess.

3 Heat the oil in a frying pan and fry the fish for 2–3 minutes until they are golden brown and crisp. Turn occasionally.

4 To make the sauce, heat the oil in a heavy frying pan and fry the onion until it is soft.

5 Add the red pepper, christophene and garlic and stir-fry for 2 minutes. Pour in the malt vinegar, then add the remaining ingredients and simmer for 5 minutes. Leave to stand for 10 minutes, then pour it over the fish. Serve hot, garnished with some lemon wedges.

COOK'S TIP
In the Caribbean, whole red snapper or red mullet are used for this dish.

SPICY FRIED CHICKEN

This crispy chicken is superb hot or cold. Served with a salad or vegetables, it makes a delicious lunch and is ideal for picnics or snacks, too.

INGREDIENTS
4 chicken drumsticks
4 chicken thighs
10ml/2 tsp curry powder
2.5ml/¹/₂ tsp garlic granules
2.5ml/¹/₂ tsp ground black pepper
2.5ml/¹/₂ tsp paprika
salt
300ml/¹/₂ pint/1¹/₄ cups milk
oil, for deep frying
50g/2oz/4 tbsp plain flour
orange slices, to garnish
salad leaves, to serve

SERVES 4–6

1 Place the chicken pieces in a bowl and sprinkle with curry powder, garlic granules, black pepper, paprika and salt. Rub the spices into the chicken, then cover and leave to marinate in a cool place for at least 2 hours, or overnight in the fridge.

2 Preheat the oven to 180°C/350°F/Gas 4. Pour enough milk into the bowl to cover the chicken and leave it to stand for a further 15 minutes.

3 Heat the oil in a large saucepan or deep-fat fryer and tip the flour on to a plate. Shake off any excess milk from the chicken and dip each piece in flour. Fry two or three pieces at a time until golden brown, but not cooked. Continue until all the chicken pieces are browned.

4 Remove the chicken pieces with a slotted spoon and place them on a baking tray. Bake in the oven for about 30 minutes. Serve hot or cold with salad leaves and garnish with orange slices.

LAMB PILAU

R ice is often cooked with meat and coconut milk. In this recipe, you can use stock instead, if you want a lighter effect.

INGREDIENTS
450g/1lb stewing lamb
15ml/1 tbsp curry powder
1 onion, chopped
2 garlic cloves, crushed
2.5ml/¹/₂ tsp dried thyme
2.5ml/¹/₂ tsp dried oregano
1 fresh or dried chilli
25g/1oz/2 tbsp butter or margarine,
plus extra for serving
600ml/1 pint/2¹/₂ cups beef or chicken
stock or coconut milk
5ml/1 tsp freshly ground black pepper
2 tomatoes, chopped
10ml/2 tsp sugar
30ml/2 tbsp chopped spring onion
450g/1lb basmati rice
spring onion strips, to garnish

SERVES 4

1 Cut the stewing lamb into cubes and place in a shallow glass or china dish. Sprinkle with the curry powder, onion, garlic, herbs and chilli and stir well. Cover loosely with clear film and leave to marinate in a cool place for 1 hour.

2 Melt the butter or margarine in a pan and fry the lamb for 5–10 minutes, on all sides. Add the stock or coconut milk, bring to the boil, then lower the heat and simmer for 35 minutes, or until the meat is tender.

3 Add the black pepper, tomatoes, sugar, spring onion and rice, stir well and reduce the heat. Make sure that the rice is covered by 2.5cm/1in of liquid and add a little water if necessary. Simmer the pilau for 25 minutes, or until the rice is cooked, then stir a little extra butter or margarine into the dish before serving. Serve garnished with spring onion strips.

THYME AND LIME CHICKEN

lthough this is not a traditional dish, it contains many of the ingredients and flavours that are characteristic of the Caribbean.

INGREDIENTS
8 chicken thighs
30ml/2 tbsp chopped spring onion
5ml/1 tsp dried or chopped fresh thyme
2 garlic cloves, crushed
juice of 1 lime or lemon
90ml/6 tbsp melted butter
salt and freshly ground black pepper
lime slices and coriander sprigs,
to garnish
cooked rice, to serve

SERVES 4

COOK'S TIP
You may need to use two limes, depending on their size and juiciness. Or, for a less sharp flavour, you can use lemons instead.

1 Put the chicken thighs in an ovenproof dish or on a baking tray skin-side down. Using a sharp knife, make a lengthways slit along the bone of each thigh. Mix the spring onion with a little salt and pepper and press the mixture into the slits.

2 Mix together the thyme, garlic, lime or lemon juice and all but 30ml/2 tbsp of the butter in a small bowl and spoon a little over each chicken thigh.

3 Spoon the remaining butter over the top. Cover the chicken loosely with clear film and leave to marinate in a cool place for several hours, or overnight in the fridge.

4 Preheat the oven to 190°C/375°F/Gas 5. Remove the clear film from the chicken and cover the dish with foil. Bake the chicken for 1 hour, then remove the foil and cook for a few more minutes to brown. Serve hot with rice and garnish with lime slices and coriander sprigs.

CARIBBEAN MUTTON CURRY

This popular national dish from Jamaica is known as Curry Goat. However, lamb or mutton can be used instead of goat meat.

INGREDIENTS
900g/2lb boned leg of mutton or lamb
50g/2oz/4 tbsp curry powder
3 garlic cloves, crushed
1 large onion, chopped
4 thyme sprigs or 5ml/1 tsp dried thyme
3 bay leaves
5ml/1 tsp ground allspice
30ml/2 tbsp vegetable oil
50g/2oz/4 tbsp butter or margarine
900ml/1½ pints/3¾ cups stock or water
1 fresh hot chilli pepper, chopped
coriander sprigs, to garnish
cooked rice, to serve

SERVES 4–6

1 Cut the meat into 5cm/2in cubes, discarding any excess fat and gristle.

2 Place the mutton or lamb, curry powder, garlic, onion, thyme, bay leaves, allspice and oil in a large bowl and mix. Marinate in the fridge for at least 3 hours, or overnight.

3 Melt the butter or margarine in a large heavy saucepan and add the seasoned mutton or lamb. Fry over a moderate heat for about 10 minutes, turning the meat frequently as it cooks.

4 Stir in the stock or water and chilli pepper and bring to the boil. Reduce the heat, cover the pan and simmer for 1½ hours, or until the meat is tender. Garnish with coriander and serve with a rice dish.

POT ROAST OF BEEF WITH RED ONIONS

he French-Caribbean tradition of marinating and spicing meat has been used to create this dish.

INGREDIENTS

1.5–1.7kg/3–4lb boned and rolled joint
of beef, such as topside or silverside
15ml/1 tbsp hoi-sin sauce
2 garlic cloves, crushed
15ml/1 tbsp spice seasoning
1 red onion, thinly sliced
¹/₂ green pepper, thinly sliced
4–5 fresh basil leaves
300ml/¹/₂ pint/1¹/₄ cups red wine
300ml/¹/₂ pint/1¹/₄ cups cold beef stock
plain flour or fine cornmeal, for dusting
30ml/2 tbsp vegetable oil
basil sprigs, to garnish
creamed sweet potatoes and okra, to serve

SERVES 6–8

COOK'S TIP
For the creamed sweet potatoes, peel then boil 900g/2lb white sweet potatoes for 30 minutes. Drain and add 50g/2oz/4 tbsp butter, a little grated nutmeg, 45ml/3 tbsp single cream, snipped chives and seasoning, then mash.

1 Untie the beef, open it out and spread it with hoi-sin sauce, garlic and half the spice seasoning. Scatter half of the onion, the pepper and a few basil leaves on top. Roll it up and re-tie with cotton string. Sprinkle with the remaining seasoning.

2 Place the meat in a bowl and add enough wine and cold stock to cover. Seal with clear film and marinate in the fridge for 8 hours, or overnight.

3 Remove the meat and roll it in the flour or cornmeal. Heat the oil in a heavy-based pan and brown the meat on all sides.

4 Lift the meat out on to a plate and pour away any excess oil. Return the meat to the pan and add the reserved marinade, onion, pepper and basil.

5 Bring to the boil, then cover and simmer gently for about 2 ½ hours, or until the beef is tender.

6 Transfer the meat to a warmed serving plate and boil the cooking liquid until it is slightly syrupy and reduced by about half. Pour it into a serving jug and serve with the meat, accompanied with creamed sweet potatoes and okra, and garnished with basil.

PORK ROASTED WITH HERBS, SPICES AND RUM

n the Caribbean, this spicy roast pork is usually barbecued and served on special occasions.

INGREDIENTS
2 garlic cloves, crushed
45ml/3 tbsp soy sauce
15ml/1 tbsp malt vinegar
15ml/1 tbsp finely chopped celery
30ml/2 tbsp chopped spring onion
7.5ml/1½ tsp dried thyme
5ml/1 tsp dried sage
2.5ml/½ tsp mixed spice
10ml/2 tsp curry powder
120ml/4fl oz/½ cup rum
15ml/1 tbsp demerara sugar
1.5kg/3–3½lb joint of pork, boned
salt and freshly ground black pepper
spring onion curls, to garnish
creamed sweet potato, to serve

FOR THE SAUCE
25g/1oz/2 tbsp butter or margarine
15ml/1 tbsp tomato purée
300ml/½ pint/1¼ cups stock
15ml/1 tbsp chopped fresh parsley
15ml/1 tbsp demerara sugar
hot pepper sauce, to taste
salt

SERVES 6–8

1 Mix together the garlic, soy sauce, vinegar, celery, spring onion, thyme, sage, mixed spice, curry powder, rum, demerara sugar and salt and pepper.

2 Open out the pork and slash the meat, without cutting through. Spread the mixture all over the pork, pressing it well into the slashes. Rub the outside of the joint with the mixture and marinate overnight.

3 Preheat the oven to 190°C/375°F/Gas 5. Roll the meat up, then tie it tightly in several places with strong cotton string to hold the meat together.

4 Spread a large piece of foil across a roasting tin and place the joint in the centre. Baste the pork with a few spoonfuls of the marinade and wrap the foil around the joint, holding in the marinade.

5 Bake in the oven for 1¾ hours, then remove the foil, baste with any of the remaining marinade and cook for 1 hour more. Check occasionally that the joint is not drying out and baste with pan juices.

6 Transfer the pork to a warmed serving dish and leave to stand in a warm place for 15 minutes before serving.

7 Meanwhile make the sauce. Pour the pan juices into a saucepan and add the butter or margarine.

8 Add the tomato purée, stock, fresh parsley, sugar, hot pepper sauce and salt to taste. Simmer gently until reduced. Serve the pork sliced, with creamed sweet potato. Garnish with spring onion curls and hand the sauce round separately.

HEARTY BEEF STEW

he brown ale gives this beef stew a real kick. Vary the amount you add to suit your taste.

INGREDIENTS

50g/2oz black-eyed beans
25g/1oz/2 tbsp butter or margarine
1 onion, chopped
675g/1½lb stewing beef, cubed
5ml/1 tsp paprika
2 garlic cloves, crushed
10ml/2 tsp ground cinnamon
10ml/2 tsp sugar
600ml/1 pint/2½ cups beef stock
150ml/¼ pint/⅔ cup brown ale
45ml/3 tbsp evaporated milk
salt and freshly ground black pepper
baby patty-pan squash, to serve

SERVES 4

1 Soak the black-eyed beans overnight, then drain and place them in a large saucepan. Cover with water and bring to the boil. Boil rapidly for a few minutes, then reduce the heat and simmer for 30 minutes, or until the beans are cooked and tender but still quite firm. Drain the beans, reserving the cooking liquid.

2 Meanwhile, melt the butter or margarine in a large saucepan and sauté the onion for a few minutes. Add the cubed beef, paprika, garlic, cinnamon and sugar and fry for about 5 minutes, until the beef is browned, stirring frequently.

3 Add the beef stock and brown ale, cover and cook for 45–60 minutes, or until the beef is almost cooked.

4 Add the milk, beans and salt and pepper and continue cooking until the beans and beef are tender. Add a little of the reserved bean liquid if the stew begins to dry out. Adjust the seasoning and serve with steamed baby patty-pan squash.

OXTAIL AND BUTTER BEANS

This is a traditional Caribbean stew: old-fashioned, economical and full of goodness. It requires patience because of the long cooking time and since there is not much meat on the oxtail it is necessary to buy a large amount. Ask your butcher to chop the oxtail unless, of course, you can use a meat cleaver!

INGREDIENTS

1.5kg/3lb oxtail, chopped into pieces
1 onion, finely chopped
3 bay leaves
4 thyme sprigs
3 whole cloves
1.75 litres/3 pints/7½ cups water
175g/6oz/1 cup dried butter beans,
soaked overnight
2 garlic cloves, crushed
15ml/1 tbsp tomato purée
400g/14oz can chopped tomatoes
5ml/1 tsp ground allspice
1 hot chilli pepper
salt and freshly ground black pepper

SERVES 4 OR MORE

1 Place the oxtail in a large heavy pan, add the onion, bay leaves, thyme and cloves and cover with water. Bring to the boil, then reduce the heat.

2 Cover the saucepan and simmer for at least 2½ hours, or until the meat is very tender, adding water whenever necessary.

3 Meanwhile, drain the butter beans, put them in a pan and cover with water. Bring the beans to the boil and simmer for 1–1¼ hours. Drain and set aside.

4 When the oxtail is cooked and the stock is well reduced, add the garlic, tomato purée, tomatoes, allspice, hot chilli pepper, salt and black pepper. Add the butter beans and simmer for a further 20 minutes. The stew should be fairly thick, but if it looks dry, add a little extra water. Adjust the seasoning and serve hot.

BARBECUED JERK CHICKEN

Jerk refers to the blend of herb and spice seasoning rubbed into meat before it is roasted over charcoal sprinkled with pepper. In Jamaica, jerk seasoning was originally used only for pork, but jerked chicken is equally good.

INGREDIENTS
8 chicken pieces
oil, for brushing
salad leaves, to serve

FOR THE MARINADE
5ml/1 tsp ground allspice
5ml/1 tsp ground cinnamon
5ml/1 tsp dried thyme
1.5ml/¼ tsp freshly grated nutmeg
10ml/2 tsp demerara sugar
2 garlic cloves, crushed
15ml/1 tbsp finely chopped onion
15ml/1 tbsp chopped spring onion
15ml/1 tbsp vinegar
30ml/2 tbsp oil
15ml/1 tbsp lime juice
1 hot chilli pepper, chopped
salt and freshly ground black pepper

SERVES 4

1 Combine all the marinade ingredients in a small bowl. Using a fork, mash them together well to form a thick paste.

2 Place the chicken pieces on a plate or board and make several lengthways slits all over the flesh. Rub the prepared marinade over the chicken pieces as well as into the slits.

3 Place the chicken pieces in a dish, cover with clear film and marinate overnight in the fridge.

4 Shake off any excess seasoning from the chicken. Brush with oil and either place on a baking sheet or on a barbecue grill, if barbecuing. Cook under a preheated grill for 45 minutes, turning often. Or, if barbecuing, light the coals and when ready, cook over the coals for 30 minutes, turning often. Serve hot with salad leaves.

COOK'S TIP
The flavour is best if you marinate the chicken overnight. Sprinkle the charcoal with aromatic herbs, such as bay leaves, if you desire even more flavour.

GREEN BANANAS AND YAM IN COCONUT MILK

ere is another way of using the popular ingredients, yams and green bananas.

INGREDIENTS

900ml/1½ pints/3¾ cups water
4 green bananas, peeled and halved
450g/1lb white yam, peeled and
cut into pieces
1 thyme sprig
40g/1½oz creamed coconut
salt and freshly ground black pepper
chopped fresh thyme and thyme
sprigs, to garnish

SERVES 3–4

1 Bring the water to the boil in a large saucepan, reduce the heat and add the green bananas and yam. Simmer gently for about 10 minutes.

2 Add the thyme, creamed coconut and seasoning. Bring back to the boil and cook over a moderate heat until the yam and banana are tender.

3 Transfer the yam and bananas to a plate with a slotted spoon and then continue cooking the coconut milk in the saucepan until it turns thick and creamy.

4 When the sauce is ready, return the fruit to the pan and heat through. Spoon into a warmed serving dish, sprinkle with chopped thyme and garnish with thyme sprigs.

COU-COU

A Barbadian speciality that goes well with flying fish but can also be served with any other fish, meat or vegetable stew.

INGREDIENTS
115g/4oz okra, topped, tailed and sliced
225g/8oz/1½ cups coarse cornmeal
600ml/1 pint/2½ cups water or
coconut milk
25g/1oz/2 tbsp butter
salt and freshly ground black pepper

SERVES 4

1 Cook the sliced okra in boiling water, seasoned with a little salt and pepper, for about 10 minutes. Drain and reserve the cooking liquid.

2 Bring half of the reserved liquid to the boil in a separate pan, add the okra and then beat in the cornmeal.

3 Cook the okra mixture on a very low heat, beating the mixture vigorously. Add the water or coconut milk, a little at a time, beating it in after each addition to avoid it sticking to the bottom of the saucepan and burning.

4 Cover and cook for about 20 minutes, beating occasionally. When the cornmeal granules are soft, the cou-cou is cooked. Cover it with foil and then a lid to keep it moist and hot, until required. Spread the top with butter before serving.

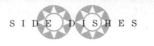
FRIED DUMPLINS

Fried Dumplins are easy to make. They are also known as "bakes" in the Caribbean and Guyana, and are often served as an accompaniment to saltfish or fried fish dishes.

INGREDIENTS
450g/1lb/4 cups self-raising flour
10ml/2 tsp sugar
2.5ml/¹/₂ tsp salt
300ml/¹/₂ pint/1¹/₄ cups milk
oil, for frying
cheese, to serve

MAKES ABOUT 10

COOK'S TIP
Dumplins are a very versatile food and they can be served as an ideal accompaniment to a lot of savoury dishes. If you prefer, however, make them as a tea-time treat to be served piping hot with butter and jam or cheese. Children in particular will love them!

1 Sift the flour, sugar and salt into a large bowl. Pour in the milk, mix, then knead the dough on a floured surface until smooth.

2 Divide the dumplin dough into ten balls, kneading each ball with floured hands for a few minutes. Press them gently with the palm of your hand to flatten them into 7.5cm/3in rounds.

3 Heat a little oil in a non-stick frying pan. Cook the dumplins in batches, reducing the heat and frying for about 15 minutes until they are golden brown, turning once.

4 Stand the dumplins on their sides for a few minutes to brown the edges, before removing them and draining on kitchen paper. Serve warm with chunks of cheese.

FRIED YELLOW PLANTAINS

When plantains are yellow they are ripe and ready to enhance most meat, fish or vegetarian dishes. The riper the plantains, the darker and sweeter they are.

INGREDIENTS
2 yellow plantains
oil, for shallow frying
finely snipped chives, to garnish

SERVES 4

1 Using a small, sharp knife, top and tail the plantains and cut them in half. Slit the skin only, along the natural ridges of each piece of plantain.

2 Ease up the edge of the skin and run the tip of your thumb along the plantains, thus lifting the skin.

3 Peel away the skin and carefully slice the plantains lengthways.

4 Heat a little oil in a large frying pan and gently fry the plantain slices for about 2–3 minutes on each side, or until they are golden brown.

5 When the plantains have turned brown and crisp, drain them thoroughly on kitchen paper and then serve them either hot or cold, sprinkled with some finely snipped chives.

CORN STICKS

This recipe produces perfect, light cornbread in a loaf tin, or makes attractive corn sticks, if you can find the moulds.

INGREDIENTS
225g/8oz/2 cups plain flour
225g/8oz/1¹/₂ cups fine cornmeal
50ml/10 tsp baking powder
2.5ml/¹/₂ tsp salt
60ml/4 tbsp demerara sugar
450ml/³/₄ pint/1⁷/₈ cups milk
2 eggs
50g/2oz/4 tbsp butter or margarine

MAKES 40 CORN STICKS

COOK'S TIP
Because there is a lot of baking powder in this recipe, the cornmeal mixture begins to rise as soon as liquid is added, so bake it straight away.

1 Preheat the oven to 190°C/375°F/Gas 5 and grease either corn stick moulds or a 900g/2lb loaf tin.

2 Sift together the flour, cornmeal, baking powder, salt and demerara sugar into a large mixing bowl.

3 Put the milk in another mixing bowl and whisk in the eggs using a hand beater. Mix together thoroughly, then stir it into the flour mixture.

4 Melt the butter or margarine in a small pan and stir it into the mixture.

5 Spoon the mixture into the moulds or tin and bake the corn sticks for 15 minutes. If you are using a loaf tin, bake the bread for 30–35 minutes, until it is golden and hollow sounding when tapped.

CARIBBEAN FRUIT AND RUM CAKE

delicious cake with a rich flavour that can be eaten at Christmas, weddings and many other special occasions. It is more famously known as Black Cake because the recipe traditionally uses burnt sugar.

INGREDIENTS
450g/1lb/2 cups currants
450g/1lb/3 cups raisins
225g/8oz/1 cup prunes, stoned
115g/4oz/²/₃ cup mixed peel
400g/14oz/2¹/₄ cups dark soft brown sugar
5ml/1 tsp mixed spice
90ml/6 tbsp rum, plus extra if needed
300ml/¹/₂ pint/1¹/₄ cups sherry,
plus extra if needed
450g/1lb/4 cups self-raising flour
450g/1lb/2 cups softened butter
10 eggs, beaten
5ml/1 tsp vanilla essence

MAKES 1 CAKE

COOK'S TIP
For a quicker preparation time, you can simmer the dried fruits in the alcohol mixture for about 30 minutes, and leave overnight.

1 Wash the currants, raisins, prunes and mixed peel, then pat them dry. Place the fruit in a food processor or blender and process until finely chopped. Transfer to a large, clean jar or bowl, add 115g/4oz of the sugar, the mixed spice, rum and sherry. Mix thoroughly and then cover with a lid and set aside for anything from 2 weeks to 3 months – the longer it is left, the better the flavour of the cake will be.

2 Stir the fruit mixture occasionally and keep it covered, adding more alcohol, if you like.

3 Preheat the oven to 160°C/325°F/Gas 3. Grease and line one 25cm/10in round cake tin using a double layer of greaseproof paper as this is a rich cake.

4 Sift the flour, and set aside. Cream together the butter and remaining sugar and beat in the eggs until the mixture is smooth and creamy.

5 Add the prepared fruit mixture, then gradually stir in the flour and vanilla essence. Mix well, adding 15–30ml/1–2 tbsp sherry if the mixture is too stiff; it should just fall off the back of the spoon, but should not be too runny.

6 Spoon the mixture into the prepared tin, cover loosely with foil and bake for about 2¹/₂ hours until the cake is firm and springy. Leave to cool in the tin overnight, then sprinkle with more rum if the cake is not to be used immediately. Wrap the cake in foil to keep it moist.

FRUITS OF THE TROPICS SALAD

Tropical fruits grow in abundance in the Caribbean and they are eaten throughout the day. This salad makes a light dessert, and a refreshing alternative to the richer baked dishes.

INGREDIENTS
1 pineapple
400g/14oz can guava halves in syrup
2 bananas, sliced
1 large mango, peeled, stoned and diced
115g/4oz stem ginger, plus
30ml/2 tbsp of the syrup
60ml/4 tbsp thick coconut milk
10ml/2 tsp sugar
2.5ml/¹/₂ tsp freshly grated nutmeg
2.5ml/¹/₂ tsp ground cinnamon
strips of coconut, to decorate

SERVES 4–6

1 Peel, core and cube the pineapple, and place it in a serving bowl. Drain the guavas, reserving the syrup, and chop. Add the guavas to the bowl with one of the bananas and the mango.

2 Chop the stem ginger and add it to the pineapple mixture.

3 Pour 30ml/2 tbsp of the ginger syrup and the reserved guava syrup into a blender or food processor and add the other banana, the coconut milk and the sugar. Blend to make a smooth creamy purée.

4 Pour the banana and coconut mixture over the fruit and add a little grated nutmeg and a sprinkling of cinnamon. Serve the fruit salad lightly chilled and decorated with strips of coconut.

BREAD AND BUTTER CUSTARD

This dessert is a truly delicious family favourite. A richer version can be made with fresh cream instead of evaporated milk. It can also be made using other dried fruit – mango works particularly well.

INGREDIENTS
15ml/1 tbsp softened butter
3 thin slices of bread, crusts removed
400g/14oz can evaporated milk
150ml/¹/₄ pint/²/₃ cup fresh milk
2.5ml/¹/₂ tsp mixed spice
45ml/3 tbsp demerara sugar
2 eggs, whisked
75g/3oz/¹/₂ cup sultanas
freshly grated nutmeg
a little icing sugar, for dusting

SERVES 4

1 Preheat the oven to 180°C/350°F/Gas 4 and lightly butter an ovenproof dish. Butter the bread and cut into small pieces.

2 Arrange the buttered bread in layers in the prepared dish.

3 Whisk together the evaporated milk and the fresh milk, mixed spice, sugar and eggs in a large bowl. Pour the mixture over the bread and butter. Sprinkle over the sultanas and leave to stand for 30 minutes.

4 Grate a little nutmeg over the top and bake in the oven for 30–40 minutes, until the custard is just set and golden. Serve the custard pudding sprinkled with some icing sugar.

APPLE AND CINNAMON CRUMBLE CAKE

This scrumptious cake has layers of spicy fruit and crumble and it is quite delicious when served warm with plenty of fresh cream.

INGREDIENTS
3 large cooking apples
2.5ml/¹/₂ tsp ground cinnamon
250g/9oz/1 cup butter
250g/9oz/1¹/₄ cups caster sugar
4 eggs
450g/1lb/4 cups self-raising flour

FOR THE CRUMBLE TOPPING
175g/6oz/³/₄ cup demerara sugar
125g/4¹/₄oz/1¹/₄ cups plain flour
5ml/1 tsp ground cinnamon
65g/2¹/₂oz/about 4¹/₂ tbsp
desiccated coconut
115g/4oz/¹/₂ cup butter

MAKES 1 CAKE

1 Preheat the oven to 180°C/350°F/Gas 4. Grease a 25cm/10in round cake tin and line the base with greaseproof paper. To make the crumble topping, mix together the sugar, flour, cinnamon and coconut in a bowl, then rub in the butter with your fingertips and set aside.

2 Peel and core the apples, then grate them coarsely. Place them in a bowl, sprinkle with the cinnamon and set aside.

3 Cream the butter and sugar in a bowl with an electric mixer, until light and fluffy. Beat in the eggs, one at a time, beating well after each addition.

4 Sift in half the flour, mix well, then add the remaining half and stir it together until the mixture is smooth.

5 Spread half the cake mixture over the base of the tin. Spoon the apples on top and scatter over half the crumble topping.

6 Spread the remaining cake mixture over the crumble and finally top with the remaining crumble topping.

7 Bake for at least 1 hour 10 minutes, covering with foil if it browns too quickly. Leave in the tin for 5 minutes, before turning out. Once cool, cut into slices.

COOK'S TIP
To make the topping in a blender or food processor, add all the ingredients and process for a few seconds until the mixture resembles breadcrumbs.

BARBADIAN COCONUT SWEET BREAD

ften made at Christmas time, this delicious coconut bread is most enjoyable with a cup of hot chocolate or a glass of fruit punch.

INGREDIENTS

175g/6oz/³/₄ cup butter or margarine
115g/4oz/²/₃ cup demerara sugar
225g/8oz/2 cups self-raising flour
200g/7oz/scant 2 cups plain flour
115g/4oz/1¹/₃ cup desiccated coconut
5ml/1 tsp mixed spice
10ml/2 tsp vanilla essence
15ml/1 tbsp rum (optional)
2 eggs
about 150ml/¹/₄ pint/²/₃ cup milk
15ml/1 tbsp caster sugar, blended with
30ml/2 tbsp water, to glaze

MAKES 1 LARGE
OR TWO SMALL LOAVES

1 Preheat the oven to 180°C/350°F/Gas 4. Grease two 450g/1lb loaf tins or one 900g/2lb tin.

2 Place the butter or margarine and demerara sugar in a large mixing bowl and sift in the flour. Rub the ingredients together with your fingertips until the mixture resembles fine breadcrumbs.

3 Add the coconut, mixed spice, vanilla essence, rum, if using, eggs and milk and mix together well with your hands. If the mixture is too dry, moisten with milk. Knead on a floured board until firm and pliable.

4 Place the mixture in the prepared loaf tin or divide it equally if using two. Glaze with sugared water and bake for 1 hour until the loave(s) are cooked. The bread is ready when a skewer comes out of the centre clean. Leave to cool, turn out of the tin, and serve sliced.

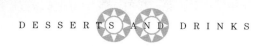

CARIBBEAN CREAM STOUT PUNCH

This is a very well-known and loved pick-me-up that is popular all over the Caribbean.

INGREDIENTS
475ml/16fl oz/2 cups stout
300ml/½ pint/1¼ cups evaporated milk
75ml/5 tbsp condensed milk
75ml/5 tbsp sherry
2–3 drops vanilla essence
freshly grated nutmeg
cinnamon sticks, to decorate

SERVES 2

1 Mix together the stout, evaporated and condensed milks, sherry and vanilla essence in a blender or food processor, or whisk them together in a large mixing bowl, until they are creamy.

2 Add a little grated nutmeg to the stout mixture and blend or whisk it again for a few minutes.

3 Chill for at least 45 minutes until really cold before pouring it into glasses and decorating it with cinnamon sticks.

ISLAND MIST FRUIT PUNCH

Refreshing, fruity glasses of punch are popular in the Caribbean. This one does not contain alcohol so it is a delicious drink for all the family to enjoy.

INGREDIENTS

2 bananas

60ml/4 tbsp ginger syrup

2.5ml/¹/₂ tsp almond essence

2.5ml/¹/₂ tsp vanilla essence

1 litre/1³/₄ pints/4 cups mango juice

750ml/1¹/₄ pints/3 cups pineapple juice

250ml/8fl oz/1 cup lemonade

freshly grated nutmeg

lemon balm and orange slices, to decorate

SERVES 3–4

COOK'S TIP
Prepare this punch up to 2 hours in advance and chill until ready to serve.

1 Peel the bananas and chop them into 1cm/¹/₂ in pieces.

2 Blend the bananas, ginger syrup and both essences in a blender or food processor until they are smooth.

3 Transfer the mixture to a large punch bowl. Stir in the mango and pineapple juices, then pour in the lemonade. Finish by sprinkling in some grated nutmeg. Serve chilled, decorated with lemon balm and orange slices.

INDEX